Learning the Word for Life

BOOK II
BREAD FOR THE WILDERNESS

Learning the Word for Life

BOOK II
BREAD FOR THE WILDERNESS

A DEVOTIONAL
DESIGNED TO HELP PEOPLE
MEMORIZE, MEDITATE & INTERNALIZE
THE WORD OF GOD

"PictureThis!" Ministries, Inc. is an evangelical, non-profit 501(c)(3) organization dedicated to serving the Christian community world wide.

Scripture taken from the New King James Version. Copyright 1979, 1980, 1982 by Thomas Nelson, Inc. Used by permission. All rights reserved. Printed in the United States of America.

"Bread... for the Wilderness"

W ebster defines a wilderness as "any barren, empty, or open area... a large, confused mass or tangle of persons or things." In the Bible, the word "wilderness" is sometimes rendered "desert" (eremos), "an unenclosed, uncultivated plain, where wild beasts roam at will."

This book is about <u>spiritual</u> wildernesses- those places or times in our lives when God seems distant, our lives feel like they are unraveling and the "wild beasts" roar. Times when prayers bounce off the ceiling. Even the word of God, our great well of encouragement, seems dry, almost a mockery to our situation. Spiritual wildernesses can be "hell on earth".

Spiritual wildernesses are inescapable. Peter warns, "Beloved, do not think it strange concerning the fiery trial which is to try you, as though some strange thing happened to you" (I Pet. 4:12). Dry places are part of the believers' turf and if, in our witnessing, we leave the impression that being a Christian is all love, peace and joy, we are not telling the whole truth. God is good but life is tough.

God used the wilderness to train our forefathers. Jesus, our Leader, started His ministry in the wilderness. The book of Hebrews' "hall of fame" has 2 categories of believers in the wilderness: those who experienced suffering- with eventual victory, and those who were tortured... "experiencing trials of mockings, scourging, chains, imprisonment, stoned, sawn in two, tempted, slain with the sword, wandered about in sheepskins, destitute, afflicted, tormented..." (Our desert places can be bad, but nothing like being sawn in two).

Yet James advises, "Count it (the wilderness) all joy." This could only be said by a crazy man or a man who had found a secret bread for the dry places. We must remember- every trial carries with it the possibility of an equal or greater benefit (the wilderness will make us bitter or better)... and the wilderness can be an **entrance** to the Promised Land. This little book is designed to help believers not just survive the dry places in life, but to come through victorious. God has provided the bread. It is up to us to eat and celebrate.

Dan & Juanene Peters

"PictureThis!" Ministries, Inc. Thousand Oaks, California

God's Design for Wildernesses

As a loving dad would do for his children, the patriarch Moses gathered Israel around him for final "Promised Land" instructions, recorded in the book of Deuteronomy. And, hoping that these children would profit by their fathers' mistakes, he carefully rehearsed the reasons for the wilderness from which they were about to emerge after 40 long years (Deut. 8:2-3). Although they were slaves in exile and we are many generations removed from that time, we would do well to examine those reasons for the wilderness.

One of the drawings from "Learning the Word for Life- Book I" (see inset) may help in "seeing" the wilderness teaching more quickly. It may also help for you to turn to Deuteronomy 8:2-3 and read it a couple of times. The sequence starts with the cloud, which you will remember, is our symbol for God. In this case "**LG**" appears on the **cloud** signifying "The Lord God" which is the beginning of Moses' dissertation. As stated in the preface of this book, the wilderness is a training ground designed by God for His people. Our irresponsible behavior may have caused us to find the "gate", but God has designed the course.

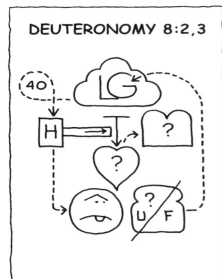

DEUTERONOMY 8:2,3

From the left side of the cloud, a **dotted line loop** encircles the number **"40"**. Training for the children of Israel required 40 years. Usually, the amount of time in the wilderness depends on the condition of the heart.

The **hammer** with the **"H"** indicates the first reason for the wilderness.

1. **Humble**. Did these Jewish **slaves** need humbling? Pride is a matter of the heart, not position or status. A story is told of a

little girl being disciplined by her mother who told her daughter repeatedly to "sit down". Finally the little girl obeyed with these words: "I may be sitting down on the outside, but on the inside I am still standing up."

Prejudice can be more than an issue of skin color; it can relate to subtle feelings of superiority involving money or stature... home owners versus the homeless, employed versus jobless. A serious and prolonged dose of a wilderness experience can destroy all status symbols. The arrow on the **handle** points to the second reason for the wilderness- shown as a capital "T".

2. **Test**. Life on planet Earth is not only "glory to glory"; it is from test to test. When your car breaks down, your spouse is screaming, or your teenager rebels, it may help to hear God saying, "testing, testing, testing." God needed to know what was in their hearts (the **heart** with a "**?**") and, whether they would keep His commands (shown as tablets). "The heart is deceitful above all things, and desperately wicked. Who can know it?", asks Jeremiah. God answers, "I the Lord, search the heart" (Jer. 17:9). God knows that we may never know the contents of our heart until the cup gets bumped.

3. **Teach**. It was <u>God</u> Who allowed them to hunger (**face with tongue hanging out**) and it was God Who gave the miraculous provision of manna ("Manna" means, "what is it?") They nor their fathers who died in the wilderness, knew what the substance was (letters "**?, U, F**"). Through all of this, God was teaching them that man does not live by bread alone (**bread** with **slash**), but by every word that proceeds from the mouth of God (**dotted line** returns to open "**G**"). God's question for all of us is, "Will you keep My commandments (act in a godly manner) when the fire gets turned up?"

Wildernesses can drive us closer or further from God; it is our choice. God's promise to us is, "I am faithful. I will never allow you to be tempted (or tested) beyond what you can handle and I will, with every temptation, provide you a way to escape." That "way" is total dependence on His word.

Voices in the Wilderness

Another wilderness example comes from the life of our Lord. As mentioned in the preface, Jesus was lead into this place of testing by the Holy Spirit; the decision to fast was His. Why? Remember the definition stated in the preface- "where wild beasts roam at will". The wilderness is full of voices: God's, ours, friends and the enemy... and it is vitally important that we recognize the source. Sometimes fasting such as Jesus did, is the surest way of discernment. Here are three tests Jesus faced and we will face, from voices in the wilderness.

The challenge of identity. Just prior to entering the wilderness, Jesus heard a clear announcement from heaven, "You are My beloved Son; in You I am well-pleased." Yet, twice the wilderness "beast" challenged that relationship. And so it is with believers today. At the moment of rebirth and possibly months after, we heard comforting assurance from our Heavenly Father. Then, as trials and testing come, we hear a different voice challenging, "Hath God said?"

The challenge of trust. Having lost the identity issue, Satan now questions, "God may have said that You were His Son, but can you trust Him? Test Him." Our temptation is worded differently: "Has God really said He would take care of you? You seem to be hungry. You have no joy in your life now-a-days. Have you noticed -your prayers are not being answered?" In the wilderness, (with a little help from the enemy) our concept of God can become skewed. We can begin to feel that He doesn't care, He is busy, mean, selfish or we have finally expended our tickets for His mercy.

The challenge of purpose. Many voices in the wilderness will point to the fast lane, to instant success. Satan suggests to Jesus, "Forget the plan. Throw Yourself over the edge, angels will pick You up and presto, You will have instant popularity." Satan's strategy does not change. He is still saying, "Just do it. Others get caught, but you live above the rules. Throw yourself and your standards down. You will be honored".

One final, important point from our Saviors' wilderness experience: Jesus was full of the word. He did not stammer, look for His concordance or a rabbi. His sword was quick and His aim was accurate. We too, must be saturated with word and know how to use it. Jesus said, "My sheep hear My voice." As we walk on with Him, His caution, "Don't go there", or "this is the way", should be a normal part of our guidance. We can't hear His voice (on a consistent basis) if His word is not in us.

Rest in the Wilderness

Our greatest hope in the wilderness is "God's Rest"- that place of repose and safety which He has designed for weary sojourners. Hebrews chapter 4 provides a perspective and description of this unique rest.

1. First of all, it is **God's** rest, His design, His idea. Unlike man's attempt at relaxation, God's rest **works**. The question, "Are we having fun yet" strikes home because, in spite of the money and planning we invest for those sacred 2 weeks, most vacations leave us more exhausted than before we left town. At best, "man's rest" is short-lived. Reality strikes and sun tans fade almost the moment we pull in our driveway. However, God's rest, like His mercy, is new every morning.

2. God's rest <u>transcends geography</u>. Rarely does that anticipated retirement cabin deliver the rest it promised. Even the second generation Israelite to whom rest was first offered, did not find God's on-going rest when he entered the Promised Land (Heb. 4:8). The Hebrew writer describes the true "gateway" to God's provision very simply: "For we who have **believed** do enter that rest (Heb. 4:3, emphasis mine). When God's word is "mixed with faith" (Heb. 3:3), rest comes... no matter where we are.

3. Strangely enough, God's rest is <u>not optional</u>. According to the Hebrew writer, "non-rest" is rooted in two sins: unbelief and rebellion. The children of Israel like us, were recipients of God's word (the "gospel" which was preached to them, Heb. 4:2) and His faithful performance. Yet when faced with a "lack", they refused to trust Him. This lack of trust, declares the Hebrew writer, amounts to rebellion. Unfortunately, too often we fall into the same sin.

This book is designed to help you memorize Scriptures VIA drawing, and the verses listed below (some of which are illustrated in this book) will help you move into God's rest. Sometimes a simple acrostic also helps. Try this.

"R" is for RELAX. Relax? In a world where evil dictators stand ready to launch weapons of mass destruction? Relax- when our adversary walks about like a roaring lion, "seeking whom he may devour"? Jesus (and later Paul) was clear regarding worry: "be anxious in nothing" (Luke 12:29, Phil. 4:6). Relax- "The Lord is my helper... what can man do to me?" (Heb. 13:6). Relax- "There is therefore now no condemnation to those who are in Christ Jesus, who do not walk according to the flesh, but according to the Spirit" (Rom. 8:1). Mix God's word with your faith and ... relax.

2. **"E"** is for ENJOY. Centuries ago, Ezra the scribe, saw a wonderful truth: "The joy of the Lord is your strength" (Neh. 8:10). At the birth of Jesus, angels announced, "Do not be afraid, for behold, I bring you good tidings of great joy which will be to all people" (Luke 2:10). Some of the more recent movies about the life of Jesus depict Him as a man full of joy! Jesus knew how to have fun even when the pressure was on, and (to find God's rest), we must follow His example. Look up and smile-God is rejoicing over you (yes, you) with singing (Zeph. 3:17).

3. **"S"** is for SATURATE. Immerse yourself in the word of God. How can we know God's will, how can we hear His voice if we do not saturate ourselves with His word? As we have referenced previously, David delighted himself in the word of God. "Blessed is the man whose delight is in the law of the Lord. Whatever he does shall prosper" (from Psa. 1:1-3). Paul counseled Timothy that the word of God makes the man of God "complete, thoroughly equipped for every good work" (II Tim. 3:17). Rest can only come when we **know** (and believe) the word of God.

4. **"T"** is for TRUST. God will always bring us to the place of test and trust. Hebrews chapter 11 makes one truth very clear: God loves faith. He loves to see us express hope and trust in Him when there is no reason for hope. Of Abraham, Paul declares, "Contrary to hope, in hope (Abraham) believed." He did not waver at the promise of God through unbelief, but was strengthened in faith giving glory to God (Rom. 4:18-20). To find God's ultimate rest, we too must choose to believe God instead of circumstances.

From Picture to Fruit- How it Works

In the "Parable of the Sower"(Mark 4), Jesus reveals 5 vital stages in Kingdom development: the Seed (the word of God), the Soil (the human spiritual heart), the Sower (anyone who teaches or evangelizes), the Process (a mystery to both the farmer and the preacher) and the Fruit (dependant primarily on our receptivity).

This seed is like no other seed as the Bible is like no other book. From Hebrews 4:12 we learn that it is "alive". It "breathes". It is the only literature in which we can spend hours reading yet find new insight when we read it again. Inside of us the word of God is a dynamic power-giving life, light and energy. God says of His own word, "it will never return void". It cannot go "home" once it is spoken until it fulfills all that God has intended.

The process is a mystery yet God has given us insight-from His word. David for instance, knew how the word "worked". In Psalm 119, he repeats 3 major steps: memorize ("I will not forget your word"), meditate ("It is my meditation all the day"), and implant ("Your word I have hidden in my heart"). David experienced fruit- the word cleanses, diverts sinning, gives life, makes wise, and provides light inside and out (just to name a few). Internalized, the written word becomes the living word.

"Learning the Word for Life" series focuses on these three points from Psalm 119- memorize, meditate and implant. To illustrate the "picture to fruit" process we will use a lesson from this book regarding "Anger Management" (see inset) based on Psalm 4:4-5. *"Be angry, and do not sin. Meditate within your heart on your bed, and be still. Offer the sacrifices of righteousness, and put your trust in the Lord".*

Now, applying the 3 steps we learned from Psalm 119, let's transition from picture to fruit.

1. **Memorize**. Although there are numerous ways to memorize Scripture (Paul suggests singing- Colossians 3:16), Jesus used a method of picturing called parables (Mark 4:30). Because God gave all of us a right brain, creative hemisphere and because "picturing" in some form is part of comprehending and remembering information, we emphasize drawing to help imprint the Scripture on the readers' mind.

2. **Meditate**. Meditation, a term and practice found in both Old and New Testaments, simply means to "mull over", reflect, to ponder, to consider. In this case, remember that all emotions including anger (the frowning face), are good- given to us by God for a purpose. However, God also gave man the unique ability to control anger. David and other writers, warn, "don't give into anger" (the word "SIN" crossed out). Instead, we are to shut up (man with tape over his mouth), go to our "bed" and meditate ("M" on heart). This would be a good time to review, even memorize other Scriptures regarding anger, such as, Psalms 37:8-9, Proverbs 14:29, 15:1, 16:32, Romans 12:19, Ephesians 4:26, 31, Colossians 3:8, and James 1:19, 20, 26. Maybe this "wrathful" event was your fault- but even if it were not, sacrifice your rights. Give them up. Better to retain a relationship than to insist on your "rights"(we are not referring here to compromising a godly standard).

3. **Implant**. Embrace this Scripture as truth. Remember, the word of God is unlike any other word. It is alive and once truly received, GOD will make it work in your life. James exhorts, "...receive with meekness the implanted word which is able to save your souls" (James 1:21). When we implant or internalize the word, we make it a part of who we are. When Mary said to Gabriel, "be it done unto me according to Your (God's) word", she became pregnant with the Word. A similar thing happens when you receive the word and truly trust God; He changes you and He changes circumstances by the power of His word. Faith demands that we believe He is and that He rewards those who trust Him. Now you are ready to get off your bed and face the (sometimes hostile) world. You are equipped with the internalized word of God. Your mind has been renewed.

Learning the word of God is for Life!

How to Use This Book

As with our first book, "Foundations", the second half of this book contains practical applications of the methodology presented thus far. All of the 26 Master Drawings in this book are constructed in a similar manner. On the page following each Master Drawing, you will find 4 Progressive Drawings which will take you step by step through the illustration as we did with Deuteronomy 8:2-3 and Psalm 4:4-5. The dotted line drawing on the page facing the Progressive Drawings is provided for you to draw each concept in the Scripture to be memorized. This is an important step because in the process of drawing a sketch on the paper, you are also inscribing the image on your brain- which greatly helps the memorization process. By the time you have traced this dotted line sketch, you have probably memorized the Scripture. Now it is time to meditate on God's word. Turn to the next page.

Backing up the Dotted Line Drawing, you will find a "Dialogue With God" page. This is where the "implanting" process begins. Ask God for revelation. As you continue to rehearse the Scripture, redraw the illustration. Wait. Several times in the book of Psalms, David exhorts the reader to "Wait on the Lord." Let your faith become active and mix with the word as you embrace God's truth. Listen. Press in to God. Remind Him of His word, "if you draw near to God, He will draw near to you" (James 4:8). As God speaks, write in the space provided. If He says nothing at the moment, set the book aside, but keep your spiritual ears tuned through the day. God WANTS to speak to you.

Let this little book be the catalyst for you. Decide now that you will develop a life-style of memorizing, meditating and implanting the word of God. You will find renewed strength and nourishment for your wilderness experience.

Develop a Life-Style of Memorizing, Meditating & Implanting God's Word!

POWER SYMBOLS

The Wilderness Bread

The Scriptures illustrated in this book are specifically designed to help in the wilderness experience described in the first part of this book. God said, "I will never leave you or forsake you." Calling on Him through His word is a way to prove- He is always there in every circumstance of life. Keep working with these verses until you **know** the voice of your Shepherd.

"Create in me a clean heart, O God, and renew a steadfast spirit within me.

Do not cast me away from Your presence, and do not take Your Holy Spirit from me.

Restore to me the joy of Your salvation, and uphold me with Your generous Spirit.

Then I will teach transgressors Your ways, and sinners shall be converted to You."

Dialogue with God

"Let us draw near with a true heart in full assurance of faith, having our hearts sprinkled from an evil conscience and our bodies washed with pure water.

Let us hold fast the confession of our hope without wavering, for He who promised is faithful.

And let us consider one another in order to stir up love and good works, not forsaking the assembling of ourselves together, as is the manner of some,

but exhorting one another, and so much the more as you see the Day approaching."

Dialogue with God

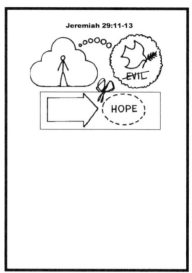

For I know the thoughts that I think toward you, says the Lord, thoughts of peace and not of evil,

to give you a future and a hope.

Then you will call upon Me and pray to Me, and I will listen to you.

And you will seek Me and find Me, when you search for Me with all your heart."

Dialogue with God

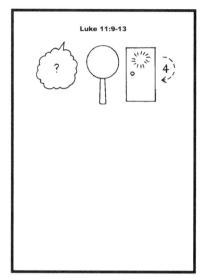

"And I say to you, ask, and it will be given to you; seek, and you will find; knock, and it will be opened to you.

For everyone who asks receives, and he who seeks finds, and to him who knocks it will be opened.

If a son asks for bread from any father among you, will he give him a stone? Or if he asks for a fish, will he give him a serpent instead of a fish? Or if he asks for an egg, will he offer him a scorpion?

If you then, being evil, know how to give good gifts to your children, how much more will your heavenly Father give the Holy Spirit to those who ask Him!"

Dialogue with God

"And do not seek what you should eat or what you should drink, nor have an anxious mind.

For all these things the nations of the world seek after, and your Father knows that you need these things.

But seek the kingdom of God, and all these things shall be added to you.

Do not fear, little flock, for it is your Father's good pleasure to give you the kingdom."

Dialogue with God

"You are a chosen generation, a royal priesthood,

a holy nation, His own special people,

that you may proclaim the praises of Him

who called you out of darkness into His marvelous light."

Dialogue with God

"He has shown you, O man, what is good:

and what does the Lord require of you

but to do justly, and to love mercy,

and to walk humbly with your God?"

Dialogue with God

"Walk worthy of the calling with which you were called.

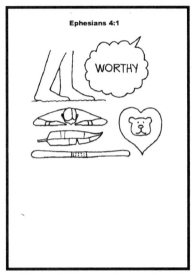

With lowliness, gentleness, long-suffering, bearing with one another in love,

endeavoring to keep the unity of the spirit

in the bond of peace."

Dialogue with God

"I beseech you therefore, brethren, by the mercies of God, that you present your bodies a living sacrifice,

holy, acceptable to God, which is your reasonable service.

And do not be conformed to this world, but be transformed by the renewing of your mind,

that you may prove what is that good and acceptable and perfect will of God."

Dialogue with God

"Have I not commanded you? Be strong and of good courage;

do not be afraid, nor be dismayed,

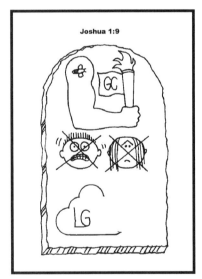

for the Lord your God is with you

wherever you go."

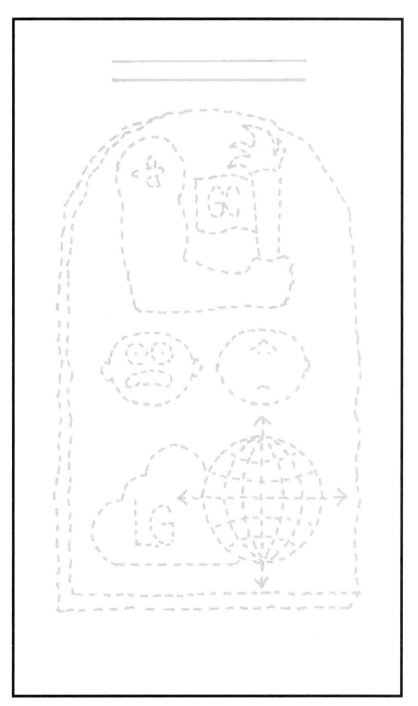

Dialogue with God

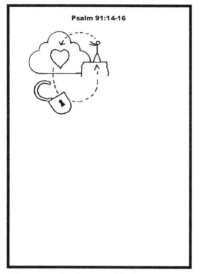

"Because he has set his love upon Me, therefore I will deliver him;

I will set him on high, because he has known My name. He shall call upon Me, and I will answer him;

I will be with him in trouble; I will deliver him and honor him.

With long life I will satisfy him, and show him My salvation."

Dialogue with God

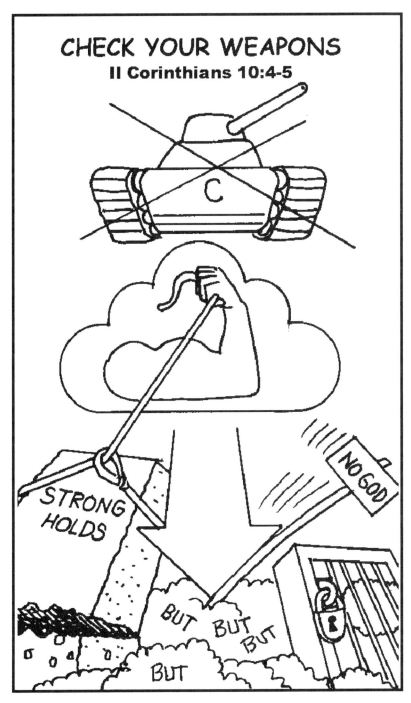

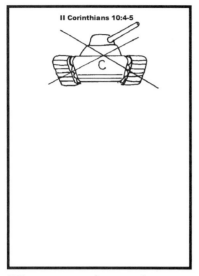

"The weapons of our warfare are not carnal

but mighty in God for pulling down strongholds,

casting down arguments and every high thing that exalts itself against the knowledge of God,

bringing every thought into captivity to the obedience of Christ."

Dialogue with God

"Let your conduct be without covetousness,

and be content with such things as you have.

For He Himself has said, 'I will never leave you nor forsake you.'

So we may boldly say: 'The Lord is my helper; I will not fear. What can man do to me?"

Dialogue with God

"My brethren, count it all joy when you fall into various trials,

knowing that the testing of your faith

produces patience. But let patience have its perfect work,

that you may be perfect and complete, lacking nothing."

Dialogue with God

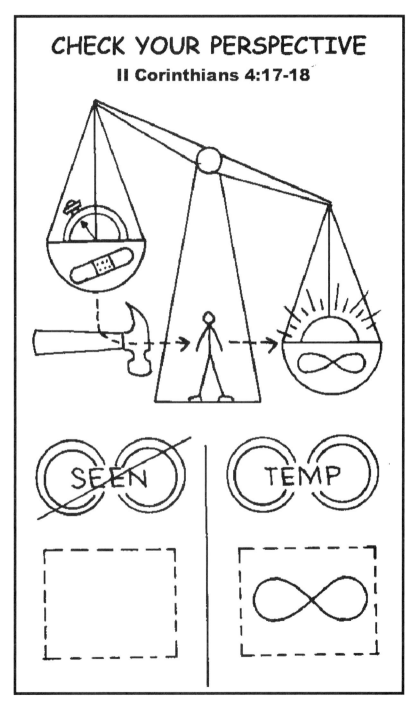

"For our light affliction, which is but for a moment,

is working for us a far more exceeding and eternal weight of glory,

while we do not look at the things which are seen, but at the things which are not seen,

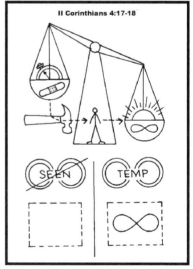

for the things which are seen are temporary, but the things which are not seen are eternal."

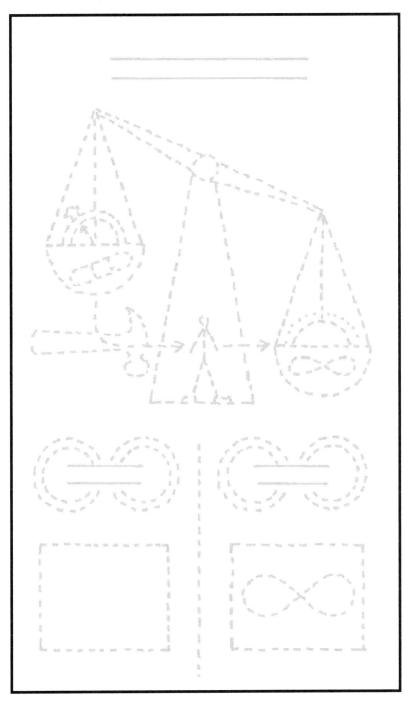

Dialogue with God

"The wisdom that is from above is first pure,

then peaceable, gentle, willing to yield,

full of mercy and good fruits, without partiality and without hypocrisy.

Now the fruit of righteousness is sown in peace by those who make peace."

Dialogue with God

"Love suffers long and is kind; love does not envy;

love does not parade itself, is not puffed up; does not behave rudely, does not seek its own,

is not provoked, thinks no evil; does not rejoice in iniquity, but rejoices in the truth;

bears all things, believes all things, hopes all things, endures all things. Love never fails."

Dialogue with God

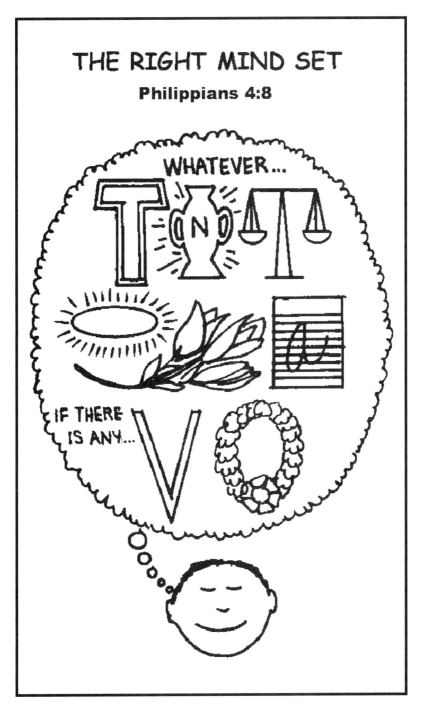

"Finally, brethren, whatever things are true, whatever things are noble,

whatever things are just, whatever things are pure,

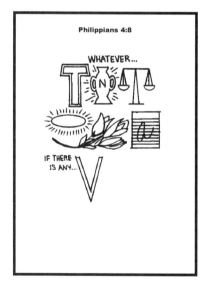

whatever things are lovely, whatever things are of good report, if there is any virtue

and if there is anything praiseworthy-meditate on these things."

Dialogue with God

"Be angry, and do not sin.

Meditate within your heart on your bed, and be still.

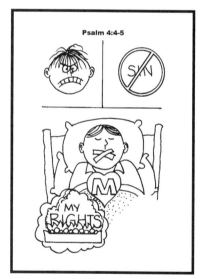

Offer the sacrifices of righteousness,

and put your trust in the Lord."

Dialogue with God

"I have learned in whatever state I am, to be content; I know how to be abased, and I know how to abound.

Everywhere and in all things I have learned both to be full and to be hungry,

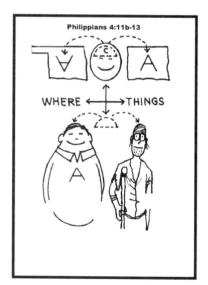

both to abound and to suffer need.

I can do all things through Christ Who strengthens me."

Dialogue with God

"Though the fig tree may not blossom, nor fruit be on the vines;

though the labor of the olive may fail, and the fields yield no food;

though the flock be cut off from the fold, and there be no herd in the stalls-

yet I will rejoice in the Lord, I will joy in the God of my salvation."

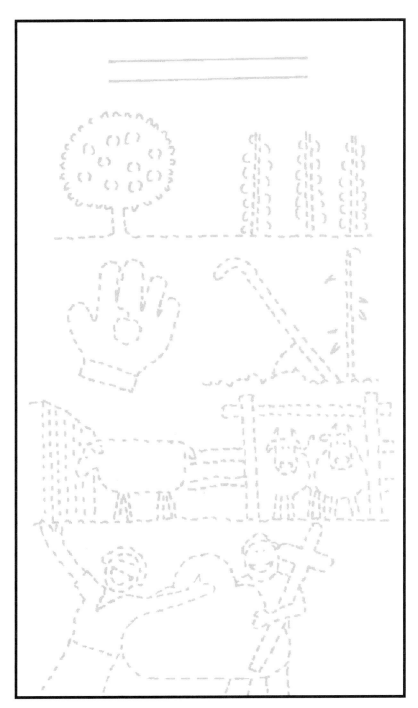

Dialogue with God

"Brethren, I do not count myself to have apprehended;

but one thing I do, forgetting those things which are behind and reaching forward to those things which are ahead,

I press toward the goal for the prize

of the upward call of God in Christ Jesus."

Dialogue with God

"You O Lord, are the portion of my inheritance and my cup,

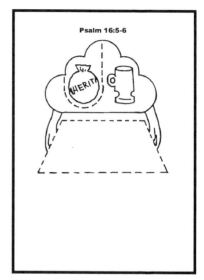

You maintain my lot.

The lines have fallen to me in pleasant places;

yes, I have a good inheritance."

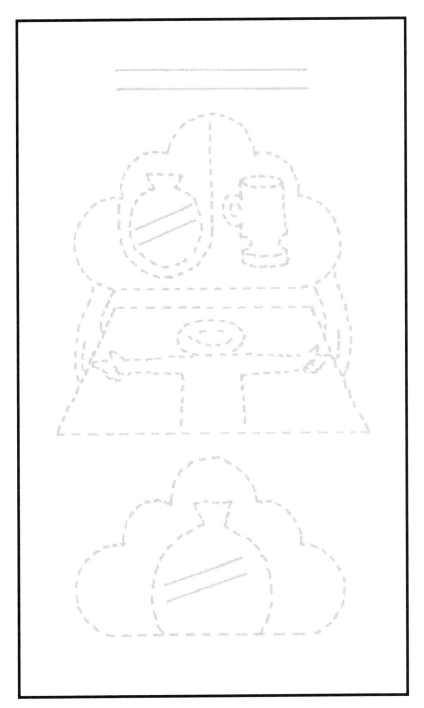

Dialogue with God

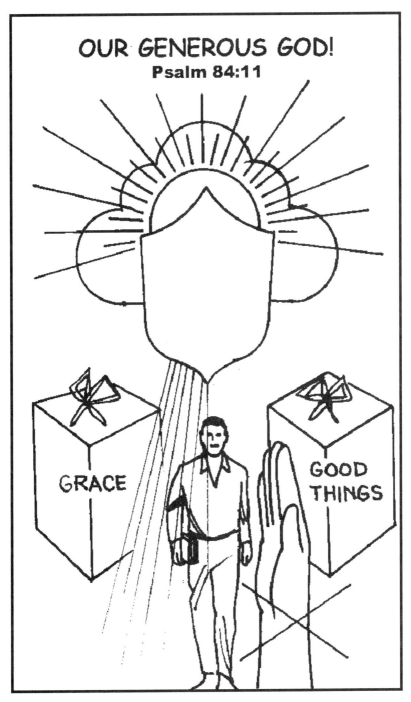

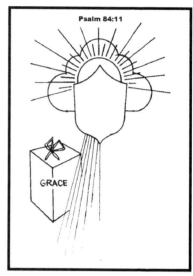

"For the Lord God is a sun and shield;

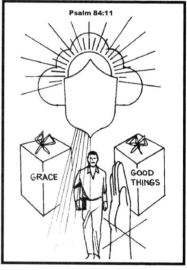

the Lord will give grace and glory;

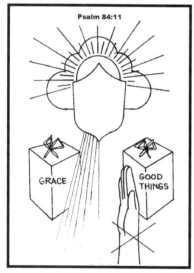

no good thing will He withhold

from those who walk uprightly."

Dialogue with God

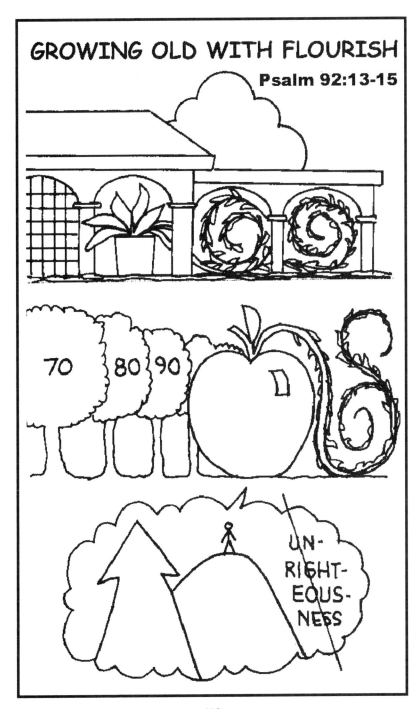

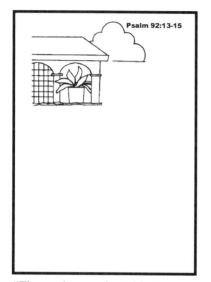

"Those who are planted in the house of the Lord

shall flourish in the courts of our God.

They shall still bear fruit in old age; they shall be fresh and flourishing,

to declare that the Lord is upright; He is my rock, and there is no unrighteousness in Him."

Dialogue with God

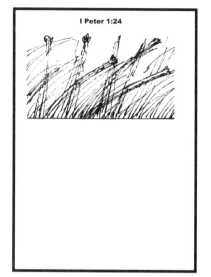

"All flesh is as grass,

and all the glory of man as the flower of the grass.

The grass withers, and its flower falls away,

but the word of the Lord endures forever."

Dialogue with God

Notes

Notes

Notes

Notes

Draw YOUR WAY THROUGH THE BIBLE!

★ EASY TO FOLLOW DOTTED-LINE ART
★ STEP BY STEP TEACHER LESSONS
★ REPRODUCIBLE STUDENT SHEETS
★ FULL YEAR PROGRAM

Each Bible book (Genesis through Revelation) is illustrated on one page. The teacher follows preprinted dotted-lines while discussing the book. Students listen, watch, & draw the same image, which maximizes retention.

Ideal for:

- *Sunday School Classes*
- *Home Bible Studies*
- *Christian Day Schools*
- *Home Schools*
- *Mission Programs*
- *Self Studies*

"PictureThis!" is available in a 2-Volume paperback set or CD Rom (Mac or PC)

DOWNLOAD A LESSON : www.bibledraw.com
CALL TOLL FREE: (888) 499-9305
OR WRITE: PictureThis! Ministries
236 Castilian Ave
Thousand Oaks, CA 91320

LEARNING THE WORD FOR LIFE!

Life Changers!

Help your friends build a lifestyle
of memorizing, meditating
& implanting the word of God.

GOD'S WORD WORKS!

CALL (888)499-9305 TO RECIEVE
MORE INFORMATION ABOUT:
★ QUANTITY DISCOUNTS
★ OTHER "PictureThis!" PRODUCTS
★ BECOMING A "PictureThis!" DISTRIBUTOR